HAPPY JOURNEY, MY FRIEND

Finding Harmony Between Your Body, Mind & Soul

KISHORE KUMAR THAKUR

Clever Fox®
PUBLISHING
Chennai • Bangalore

CLEVER FOX PUBLISHING
Chennai, India

Published by CLEVER FOX PUBLISHING 2025

ISBN: 978-93-7500-927-6

CONTENTS

FOREWORD

by Shivani Modi, Co-founder, Ceekr

I have known Kishoreji for many years now. He was part of Ceekr's very first batch when we launched the Mind Mastery classes. A gentle, quiet presence, he carried a depth that was immediately felt. We knew he was a senior and accomplished coach, and it felt like a privilege to have him learning with us. What stood out most, even then, was his hunger for learning and the clarity of his insights.

Over time, I watched him change. Slowly, quietly, steadily — he began to grow into himself more fully. I saw the very journey he writes about in this book unfolding within him. the push of the Mind, the strain of the Body, the whispers of the Soul… and finally, the arrival of the Coach — the presence that ties everything together. I saw his health improve, his inner balance deepen, and his professional practice flourish.

He embraced ancient wisdom — from the scriptures, from Mind Mastery, from his own lived experiences — not as concepts, but as disciplined, deliberate practice. In a world that often celebrates achievement at the cost of well-being, Kishoreji demonstrated something rare: **that true achievement can be holistic.** When the inner life strengthens, the outer life naturally blooms.

What he has created here is much more than a fable.

It is a mirror.
A companion.
A gentle conversation.

As I read the manuscript, I found myself on a journey — a journey inward, a journey of reflection, a journey of remembering what truly matters. I recognized so many moments: the mind running ahead, the body struggling to keep pace, and the soul waiting patiently for me to pause and choose differently.

The book carries a rhythm of its own. Each page invites you to slow down, to breathe, to absorb. It feels like spending a summer afternoon in quiet reflection — unhurried, spacious, and deeply nourishing.

I believe every reader will find themselves somewhere in these pages.
There is something here for everyone.

As I read, names and faces kept coming to mind — people I wanted to share this beautiful, profound, and quietly riveting story with.

This is a book to be read slowly.
To be breathed in.
To be felt.

Let it meet you exactly where you are.
Let it remind you of the parts of yourself you may have left behind.
Let it help you return — gently, wholly — to your own inner harmony.

I am grateful to Kishoreji for bringing this story into the world. And I am honoured to introduce it to you.

– Shivani

ABOUT THE FOREWORD WRITER

Shivani Modi is the Co-founder of **Ceekr**, www.ceekr.com an organization dedicated to advancing personal transformation, inner mastery, and conscious living. With extensive experience in the fields of self-awareness and human potential development, she has played a significant role in shaping programs that integrate ancient wisdom traditions with modern psychological and contemplative practices.

At Ceekr, Shivani leads initiatives focused on mental resilience, emotional clarity, and the cultivation of presence. Her work has touched thousands of learners, including leaders, professionals, and individuals seeking a deeper understanding of themselves and their inner world.

Known for her composed presence and insightful guidance, Shivani brings a refined blend of intuition, structure, and depth to her teaching. Her contribution to this book reflects her long-standing commitment to helping individuals strengthen their inner foundation and live with greater awareness and harmony.

Shivani continues to expand Ceekr's mission of elevating consciousness through education, community, and practice.

PREFACE

This book began as a quiet conversation within me.
Between the part of me that wanted to achieve, the part that longed to rest, and the part that simply wanted to *be.*
It all started one evening while I was watching the Hindi Bollywood movie *Zindagi Na Milegi Dobara.*
Three friends — full of life, curiosity, and courage — set out on an adventure together. As I watched their laughter, their fears, their growth, a question quietly arose in my heart:

"What if one of them were left behind? Would the others still be able to enjoy the journey?"
That thought lingered long after the film ended.
I realized that our own lives are a lot like that journey — filled with moments of excitement and discovery, but also the constant risk of disconnection.
Because we too travel with three companions — **our Body, our Mind, and our Soul.**

When they walk together, life feels complete.
But when one of them is left behind, even the most beautiful path begins to lose its color.

And that is how this book was born — as a reflection on what happens when our three inner friends drift apart, and how we can help them reunite.

🌿 The Spark of Awareness

Over the years, as I coached leaders, professionals, and seekers, I noticed something universal.
No matter how successful or strong people appeared, there was often a quiet misalignment inside — the Body tired, the Mind restless, the Soul unheard.

I began to see that the essence of coaching, and perhaps of living itself, is not about striving harder but about traveling *together* — about helping these three friends move in rhythm again.

🌸 The Journey of Three Friends

I chose to tell this story as a fable — because sometimes truth reaches deeper when it arrives softly.
It's the story of our shared humanity: of ambition, fatigue, rediscovery, and grace.
The Body symbolizes energy and action.
The Mind represents logic and leadership.
The Soul holds purpose and peace.
And the Coach — appearing later — is the quiet awareness within each of us, patiently waiting for us to pause and listen.

Through their journey, I invite you to reflect on your own — not as a reader, but as a fellow traveller.

🌼 An Invitation

This is not a book to be read quickly.
It's a journey to be experienced slowly — one that asks for your presence more than your attention.

You may find yourself in one of these friends. You may even notice when one of them within you feels left behind.
When that happens, pause. Smile. Listen.
That moment of awareness is your reunion.

Because life's true adventure isn't just about seeing new places — it's about keeping your inner companions together as you walk.
So take a deep breath, open the first page, and begin.
Not towards a destination, but towards harmony.

Happy Journey, my friend.

– Kishore Kumar Thakur

INTRODUCTION

by the Author

Every journey begins with movement,
but the most meaningful journeys begin with awareness.

This book is about a journey we are all already on —
the quiet, every day journey within ourselves.

A journey where our **Mind**, **Body**, and **Soul** walk together
not as separate forces,
but as companions.

Over the years, through coaching and conversations with leaders, seekers, and friends, I noticed something subtle yet universal:

We often live with parts of ourselves out of sync.

The mind races ahead with ideas, fears, and expectations.
The body tries to keep pace, bearing stress and fatigue.
And the soul — the gentlest part of us — waits patiently for us to slow down and listen.

This book grew out of that observation.

It is a simple story —
a fable, a reflection,
a conversation between three lifelong friends who set out on a journey together
and discover what happens when they drift apart…
and how they find their way back to harmony.

Happy Journey, My Friend is not meant to be read quickly.
It is meant to be experienced.

Each chapter invites you to pause, reflect, and reconnect with a part of yourself you may have rushed past in the busyness of life.

This is a book about:

- listening deeply
- living consciously
- honouring your inner wisdom
- and walking gently with yourself

My hope is that you meet your own Mind, Body, and Soul within these pages —
not as concepts,
but as companions who have always been with you.

This is your journey too.

And I am grateful to walk a part of it with you.

– Kishore Kumar Thakur

PART I

THE BEGINNING: WHEN THE JOURNEY FEELS NEW

CHAPTER 1

THE DEPARTURE: SETTING OUT TOGETHER

The day was clear when the three friends first began their journey. The road curved through golden fields, kissed by the morning light. Everything ahead felt wide and possible — as though the world itself had opened its arms in welcome.

The **Body** walked with a confident stride. Every movement was filled with strength and purpose.
The **Mind** followed closely, holding maps, making plans, calculating routes and distances.
The **Soul** moved lightly behind them, unhurried, smiling at the beauty in small things — the rhythm of wind, the distant song of a bird, the way sunlight played across their path.

There was no destination, not yet.
It was enough just to move — together.

The First Steps

"Where shall we go first?" asked the Mind, scanning the horizon.

"Anywhere!" said the Body, stretching its arms wide. "I've been waiting to move for so long. I want to climb, run, dance, and feel the wind on my skin."

The Soul smiled gently. "Then let us walk with curiosity. Every path teaches something."

The Mind looked amused. "That's all well and good, but we can't just wander forever. We need a plan — milestones, perhaps."

The Soul chuckled softly. "Milestones are fine, as long as we don't forget to enjoy the stones along the way."

The Body laughed, breaking the tension. "You two — always balancing each other. One wants a plan; the other wants peace. I'll keep us moving so both of you get your way."

And so they began — one thinking, one feeling, one simply being.
The perfect trinity.

The Joy of Togetherness

Days passed like gentle waves.
They explored new valleys, tasted the sweetness of fresh fruit, sang songs to the stars, and shared stories beside the campfire.

Each friend had a role to play.
The Body found joy in motion — lifting, building, exploring.
The Mind found joy in meaning — understanding, analysing, connecting.
The Soul found joy in silence — breathing, watching, simply being.

Every morning, they greeted the dawn with gratitude.
The Mind would whisper, "Let's make today meaningful."
The Body would add, "Let's make it lively."
And the Soul would complete the circle, "Let's make it peaceful."

Together, they created harmony — a rhythm that felt effortless, like a perfectly tuned melody.

The Mind loved the Body's strength and reliability.
The Body admired the Mind's clarity.
And both found quiet comfort in the Soul's stillness.

For a while, life was simple — and in that simplicity, it was perfect.

The Promise

One evening, as they sat under a wide, starlit sky, the Soul spoke softly. "Let us make a promise," it said.

The Mind looked up from its notes. "A promise?"

"Yes," said the Soul. "That no matter what happens — success, struggle, storms, or silence — we will walk together. Always."

The Body smiled. "I like that. Together, we can handle anything."

The Mind nodded thoughtfully. "Agreed. But to stay together, we must communicate. If one feels tired or lost, the others must notice."

The Soul nodded. "Yes — because this journey isn't about how far we go, but how well we stay connected."

They joined hands — one of muscle, one of thought, one of light — and sealed the promise with quiet laughter.

The fire crackled. The stars watched.

And the road ahead, unseen but certain, waited patiently for them to continue.

The First Glimpse of Difference

The next morning, they walked again — the Body energetic, the Mind focused, and the Soul quietly humming a tune.

But as the day grew hotter, a small difference began to show.
The Body wanted to rest, feeling the sun heavy on its shoulders.
The Mind, however, insisted, "Let's keep going. The next village can't be far."
The Soul said nothing — just observed with calm curiosity.
The Body hesitated, but pushed forward anyway. It didn't want to break the promise on the very first day.
And as they walked on, the Soul noticed something subtle — the Body's breath had become shallow, the Mind's thoughts sharper, and the silence between them thinner.

It was still harmony, yes — but slightly stretched.

The Soul smiled inwardly. "Even in friendship, balance needs awareness," it thought. "Let's see how long they remember to listen."

The Night Whisper

That night, while the Body slept and the Mind dreamed of maps, the Soul whispered into the darkness:
"Dear friends, may we remember that togetherness is not walking at the same speed.
It's listening when one slows down."

And the stars seemed to nod in agreement.

Coach's Journal

When I think of beginnings — of new goals, new relationships, or new journeys — I'm reminded of how easy it is to start with enthusiasm and clarity.

At the beginning, our **Body** is eager, our **Mind** is focused, and our **Soul** is hopeful.
We set out with energy, discipline, and a sense of purpose.

But beginnings are also fragile.
We assume that alignment, once achieved, will last on its own.
In truth, harmony must be *recreated* every day.
In coaching, I often meet people at the "departure stage" — full of excitement, yet unaware of how easily connections can drift.
Their challenge isn't commitment, but *continuity*.

The key is not to chase balance, but to **cultivate awareness** — to keep checking in with each part of yourself.

Ask:

"How's my Body feeling?"
"What's my Mind thinking?"
"What's my Soul whispering?"

Because awareness, not willpower, is what keeps the journey joyful.

Pause & Reflect

- When I begin something new — a project, a goal, a change — which part of me takes the lead?
- How do I check if my Body, Mind, and Soul are aligned before I start moving?
- What promise do I want to make to myself for this journey ahead?

Try this:

Before you start your day tomorrow, sit for a minute in silence.
Place your hand on your heart and take three slow breaths.

With each breath, silently greet each of your inner friends:

"Good morning, Body."
"Good morning, Mind."
"Good morning, Soul."

That's all it takes to begin in harmony.

CHAPTER 2

THE FIRST MILES: THE THRILL OF DISCOVERY

The morning sun broke over the horizon, painting the path in gold.
The Body stretched with delight, feeling the pulse of strength flow through every muscle.
The Mind stood alert, eager to move forward, already mapping new directions.
The Soul, still quiet from the dawn, watched with serene joy.

The first few miles were pure adventure.
Every turn offered a new vista — a field of flowers here, a distant hill there, a stream whispering its way through smooth stones.
The friends laughed often, sang loudly, and stopped only to marvel at the beauty of the world around them.
There was no hurry, no agenda — just movement and wonder.
Every step felt like progress, every moment like discovery.

The Call of Achievement

One afternoon, they came across a tall hill.
It wasn't too high, but it stood out against the horizon, calling silently to them.

"Let's climb it!" said the Mind, eyes bright. "From the top, we can see where we're headed next. It'll give us a sense of direction."

The Body agreed eagerly. "Perfect! A little challenge keeps me alive."

The Soul smiled. "Yes, but remember — the hill is not the point. The climb is."
They started together, laughing and pushing forward.
The Body led the way, steady and determined.
The Mind measured each step, pacing their climb.

And the Soul whispered encouragement in the pauses between breaths.

When they finally reached the top, the Mind looked around in triumph. "See?" it said proudly. "Now we know the terrain ahead — the valley, the river, even the distant mountain. If we keep this pace, we can reach there by next week."

The Body beamed, proud of its endurance.
But the Soul only looked at the horizon and said softly, "And yet, from up here, the path behind looks just as beautiful."

The Mind frowned slightly, half listening. "Yes, yes… but forward is progress. We must keep moving!"
The Body nodded in excitement, feeling the rush of momentum.
And so, without resting, they began their descent — quickly, almost eagerly, already planning the next climb.

The Beginning of Hurry

The next few days were a blur of motion.
The Body felt strong, but the pace was relentless.

The Mind was thrilled — the world was full of new places to conquer.
And the Soul… the Soul began to fall silent.

Whenever the Soul tried to speak — to pause, to reflect, to appreciate — the Mind interrupted gently, "Later. Let's just reach the next point first."

At first, the Soul smiled and agreed. But deep inside, it knew what was happening.

The joy of discovery had quietly turned into a race for completion.
The journey was no longer about wonder; it was about distance.

One evening, as they walked through a quiet forest, the Body stopped.
"I think I need to rest," it said. "My feet ache, and the air feels heavy."

The Mind hesitated, then replied, "Just a little more. We'll rest after we cross the river ahead. If we stop now, we'll lose time."

The Soul whispered softly, "Time is not lost when it's used for rest."

But the Mind didn't hear. It was already calculating the next sunrise.

A Night by the Fire

They made camp that night beside the river. The stars shimmered above, and the water sang softly to the rocks.

The Body, exhausted, fell asleep almost instantly.
The Mind stayed awake, scribbling ideas in the sand — routes, timings,plans.
The Soul sat beside the fire, watching the flames dance.

After a while, the Soul spoke gently.
"You seem restless tonight."

The Mind looked up. "Not restless. Just… prepared. We've done so well already, but we could go further if we plan properly. We can't waste this momentum."

The Soul nodded. "Momentum is useful, yes. But tell me — do you still remember why we began?"

The Mind frowned. "Of course — to explore, to experience, to grow."

The Soul smiled. "Yes. And are we still doing that — or are we just moving because we're afraid to stop?"

The question lingered in the cool air.
The Mind didn't answer. It only stared at the map drawn in sand — a map that suddenly seemed endless.

The First Shadow of Imbalance

By morning, the Body was sore. It said nothing, unwilling to slow the others down.
The Mind was eager to start early. "Let's move before the sun gets too hot," it insisted.
The Soul walked silently behind, watching, waiting.

As they moved through the valley, the Body's pace began to falter.
The Mind grew impatient. "Come on! You're slowing us down."
The Body replied softly, "I'm just tired. I need a moment."

The Mind sighed. "You always say that when we're close to progress."
The Soul finally spoke, its tone firm but calm.
"Progress is not when we move fast — it's when we move *together*."

The Mind turned, startled. "You don't understand — if we stop too often, we'll never reach anywhere!"

The Soul looked at the Mind with gentle eyes. "And if we don't stop at all, we might reach everywhere — but lose ourselves on the way."
A silence followed. Even the wind seemed to pause, listening.
The Body took a deep breath and whispered, "Maybe both of you are right. Let's find a pace we can all live with."

And for the first time, the Mind looked at the Body — really looked — and saw the strain.
Its voice softened. "Alright. Let's rest here for a while."

The Soul smiled. "Good. For rest is also part of the journey."

🏵 Harmony Restored — For Now

They sat beneath a tree by the riverside. The Body stretched, the Mind rested its thoughts, and the Soul hummed a quiet tune.

The sunlight filtered through the leaves, and for a brief moment, everything was still again.

The Body, Mind, and Soul — three travelers rediscovering balance through awareness.

The Mind looked up at the clouds drifting lazily overhead and smiled. "Maybe the Soul's right," it said softly. "Maybe progress isn't a straight line."

The Body chuckled. "Good thing — because I prefer curves."
They all laughed.
For now, harmony had returned.

But somewhere in the distance, beyond the gentle laughter, the wind carried a quiet reminder:

"The faster we move, the harder it becomes to listen."

💭 Coach's Journal

The thrill of discovery is powerful.
In the early stages of any pursuit — a project, a dream, or even self-growth — excitement fuels us. We want to see results, make progress, move faster.

But often, **the moment we start to measure joy, we begin to lose it.**
I've seen this in many of my coaching conversations.
What starts as curiosity soon turns into comparison.

What begins with meaning soon becomes measurement.
And that shift — subtle but deep — takes us away from the very essence of why we began.

The **Mind** is wired to plan, to achieve, to organize. That's its gift.
The **Body** wants to experience and participate. That's its energy.
And the **Soul** wants to witness and understand. That's its wisdom.

When these three travel in balance, discovery becomes joy.
When one dominates, joy turns into performance.

So, the next time you find yourself rushing through something you once loved — pause. Ask yourself:

"Am I still curious, or am I only counting?"

That question can bring you back home.

🌼 Pause & Reflect

- What excites me most about my current journey — the experience or the outcome?
- Where in my life am I rushing ahead without listening to my Body or Soul?
- What would it look like to move at a pace that honors all parts of me?

Try this:

Spend 10 minutes today doing something you enjoy — but slowly.
Sip your tea without multitasking.
Walk without headphones.
Breathe without purpose.
Let your Mind, Body, and Soul share the moment.

That's how you rediscover the *thrill of discovery* — without losing yourself in it.

CHAPTER 3

THE FIRST ARGUMENT: THE CRACK APPEARS

The days of laughter and easy rhythm were behind them. They still walked together, yes, but something had shifted — softly, invisibly — like a gentle crack beneath a smooth surface.

At first, no one noticed.
The Body still walked, the Mind still thought, and the Soul still smiled.
But their steps no longer matched.

The Body moved slower, weighed down by fatigue.
The Mind raced ahead, restless and ambitious.
The Soul drifted behind, quiet and contemplative.

They were still on the same road, but no longer on the same journey.

🌿 The First Sign of Distance

It began one afternoon under a blazing sun.
The Body stopped suddenly, leaning against a tree, breath heavy.
"I need to rest," it said quietly.

The Mind turned sharply. "Rest? Again? We rested just yesterday!"

The Body frowned. "Yes, but I'm tired. You keep increasing our pace. You don't see what this is doing to me."

The Mind crossed its arms, impatient. "If we slow down every time you feel tired, we'll never reach anywhere. There's so much to see, so much to achieve. You'll thank me later."

The Soul, who had been watching silently, spoke in a calm tone.
"Perhaps both of you are right — but neither is listening."

The Body sighed. "I listen every day. I listen to pain, to pressure, to the constant push."

The Mind snapped, "And I listen to worry! To the fear of falling behind, of wasting time, of not being enough."

A long silence followed. The road stretched ahead, shimmering in the heat.
Even the breeze seemed to hold its breath.

The Argument Grows

By evening, they walked again — but the silence between them was no longer peaceful.
It was filled with unspoken resentment.
The Body's steps were heavy.

The Mind's thoughts were loud.
The Soul's heart was aching quietly.

Finally, the Body broke the silence. "You don't understand what it's like," it said to the Mind. "You dream, plan, think — but I'm the one carrying it all."

The Mind retorted, "And without me, you'd wander without purpose! I'm the one giving direction."

The Soul intervened softly, "Purpose without presence is just movement without meaning."

The Mind turned sharply. "Oh, please. You always say things that sound beautiful but mean nothing when we need action!"

The Soul looked down. "Maybe beauty is action — the kind that heals instead of hurries."

The Body looked from one to the other. "Stop it, both of you. We made a promise to walk together."

But the promise felt distant now — like an echo of laughter they could no longer hear.

The Breaking Point

The next morning, they woke before dawn.
The Mind insisted on an early start. "We can reach the next city by evening if we push a little harder."

The Body groaned but followed. The Soul walked in silence, watching the sky slowly turn from pink to gold.

By midday, the heat grew unbearable. The Body stumbled.
"I can't," it whispered. "My legs won't move."

The Mind turned, frustration spilling out. "You're always slowing us down! We could've covered twice this distance by now!"

The Body, hurt and weary, said softly, "You talk of distance. I talk of strength. What use is one without the other?"

The Soul stepped forward, placing a gentle hand between them.
"Stop. Listen to what's happening. You're not fighting each other — you're fighting yourselves."

But the Mind wasn't ready to hear.
"I don't have time for this," it said coldly. "If you both want to stop, fine. I'll go ahead."

And before the Body or Soul could respond, the Mind turned and walked away — fast, determined, refusing to look back.

The Silence After Separation

The Body sank to the ground, trembling with exhaustion.
The Soul sat beside it, wrapping its presence around the Body like a blanket of stillness.

For a long time, neither spoke.
Only the sound of the wind moving through the grass filled the air.

Finally, the Body whispered, "Do you think the Mind will come back?"

The Soul smiled faintly. "Eventually. It always does. But not until it tires of its own noise."

The Body closed its eyes. "It hurts. Not just the walking — but the way we stopped seeing each other."

The Soul placed a hand on the Body's shoulder. "That's how disconnection begins — not with distance, but with blindness."

The Body nodded slowly. "Then what do we do now?"

The Soul looked toward the horizon where the Mind had disappeared. "We wait. And while we wait, we rest. Healing begins when one part stops fighting and starts listening."

The Body exhaled deeply, as though releasing a weight it didn't know it carried.
The Soul closed its eyes and whispered a prayer — not for reunion yet, but for patience.

Meanwhile, the Mind

The Mind walked quickly, half angry, half afraid.

It convinced itself that it didn't need the others. "I'll manage alone," it muttered. "I've done most of the work anyway."

But as the day wore on, the noise inside grew louder — thoughts colliding, questions echoing, doubts whispering.

Without the Body, the Mind began to lose rhythm. Without the Soul, it lost clarity.
It was thinking faster than ever — and yet, nothing made sense.

When night fell, the Mind stopped near a hill and sat down, suddenly aware of the emptiness.

The stars above looked unfamiliar, the silence almost unbearable.

For the first time, the Mind felt alone — not just physically, but deeply.
And in that stillness, a single thought rose softly, painfully clear:

"Maybe I didn't leave them behind. Maybe I left myself."

The Soul's Reflection

Far away, the Soul stirred awake.
In the deep stillness of the night, it could feel the faint pulse of the Mind — restless, lonely, searching.

The Soul whispered into the darkness, though it knew the Mind couldn't hear yet:

"You'll come home soon, my friend. You'll realize that no thought is worth losing your wholeness for.

And when you do, we'll be waiting — not to judge, but to begin again."

The Body turned in its sleep and smiled faintly, as though it had heard the Soul's words in a dream.

Coach's Journal

Every relationship — even the one we have with ourselves — has moments of tension.
Moments when our **Mind** races ahead, chasing goals, while our **Body** struggles to keep up, and our **Soul** quietly waits for balance to return.

The argument between these three isn't a failure — it's a signal.
It tells us that one part of us has taken over too much space, too much control.

I've seen this often in coaching conversations.
Leaders who achieve everything on paper, yet feel empty inside.
Professionals who ignore fatigue until burnout becomes their language.
Dreamers who lose joy in the name of discipline.

When our inner friends stop communicating, disconnection begins.
But here's the hope — **awareness rebuilds connection faster than effort ever can.**

It's okay if your Mind has gone too far ahead. It's okay if your Body is tired. It's okay if your Soul feels distant.
All three are still yours.
They are waiting — patiently — for you to listen again.

The healing begins not when we find the "right" pace, but when we pause long enough to remember that we're walking the same road.

Pause & Reflect

- Where in my life am I pushing forward without listening to my body or my heart?
- What am I afraid will happen if I slow down?
- Which part of me — Body, Mind, or Soul — feels unheard right now?

Try this:

Take five minutes today to write a small letter — from your Body to your Mind, or from your Mind to your Soul.
Let them speak honestly. Don't censor, don't analyze.
Just listen.

Sometimes, the most powerful reconciliation begins not with action, but with awareness.

PART II

THE SEPARATION: WHEN LIFE FALLS OUT OF SYNC

CHAPTER 4

THE LOST FRIEND: WHEN ONE FALLS BEHIND

Morning came softly, but something felt different.
The sunlight no longer carried the warmth of promise — it fell cold across the path.
The road was the same, yet emptier.

The Mind was walking ahead, eyes fixed on the distant horizon.
The Soul followed slowly, lost in thought.
And the Body… was missing.

For the first few miles, neither noticed.
The Mind was too focused on reaching the next milestone, and the Soul — though aware of an emptiness — hoped it was just distance.

But as the wind grew quieter and the footsteps behind stopped echoing, the Soul knew.
It stopped walking.

"Where's the Body?" it whispered softly.

The Mind turned, impatient. "Probably lagging behind again. We can't stop every time it needs a break."

The Soul's eyes filled with concern. "No, Mind. This feels different. I can't feel its rhythm anymore."

The Mind sighed, scanning the path. "It'll catch up. It always does."

But deep down, even the Mind wasn't sure.

🌿 The Place Where the Body Stopped

Far behind them, under the shade of an old banyan tree, the Body sat silently.
Its breathing was shallow, its shoulders heavy.

The road had been too long, too fast, too demanding.
Every muscle ached. Every breath felt like an effort.

It looked at the dust-covered footprints ahead — the ones it had made with the Mind and Soul — and tears welled up.

"I wanted to go on," it whispered to no one. "But I just couldn't anymore."
It wasn't anger that the Body felt — it was sadness.
Sadness of being unheard.

"I carried them both," it murmured. "Their dreams, their worries, their plans… I held them all."
It touched its chest gently. "But who was holding me?"

The Body leaned back against the tree and closed its eyes.
For the first time in a long time, it stopped trying to move.

🏵 The Mind's Denial

Ahead on the trail, the Mind was restless.

It tried to ignore the discomfort growing inside — that uneasy awareness that something was missing.

The Soul's silence made it harder to pretend.
Finally, the Soul spoke softly.
"Mind… we need to go back."

The Mind snapped, "Go back? After all this distance? We can't afford that. We've worked too hard."

The Soul's voice remained calm. "What's the use of going forward if we've lost a part of ourselves along the way?"

The Mind stopped walking. The words lingered.
It looked ahead — wide valleys, inviting and open — but suddenly, they didn't look like freedom anymore. They looked lonely.

It looked back — at the winding road fading into the distance.

The Mind took a deep breath. "Alright. Let's go back."

The Soul smiled faintly. "Thank you. You just chose connection over achievement."

The Return

The journey back was harder than expected.
Without the Body's strength, the Mind and Soul struggled to keep their pace.
The Mind began to feel fatigue — something it had rarely noticed before.
The Soul walked slowly, patient, steady.

When they finally reached the banyan tree, they saw the Body sitting there, eyes closed, face peaceful but pale.

The Mind ran forward. "Body! There you are! What happened? Why did you stop?"

The Body opened its eyes slowly. "Because I couldn't go on."

The Mind knelt beside it. "You should've said something."

The Body looked at it sadly. "I did. You just weren't listening."
The Soul came closer, its voice tender.
"We're here now. Rest, dear friend. You've carried us for so long."

The Body's eyes softened. "I missed you both."

The Mind looked down, guilt pressing heavy on its chest. "I thought I was helping us by moving faster."

The Soul placed a hand on the Mind's shoulder. "Sometimes the greatest progress is the pause that heals."

🌙 The Night of Healing

They camped there that night under the banyan tree.
For the first time in weeks, they didn't talk about the next destination.
They simply sat together — breathing, listening, and remembering.

The Body felt warmth returning to its limbs.
The Mind began to quiet its endless thoughts.
The Soul smiled softly, sensing harmony returning, even if faintly.

After a long silence, the Body spoke. "I realized something while you were gone. I've always carried both of you — your worries, your desires — but I never asked to be cared for. I thought my job was only to endure."

The Soul nodded. "Endurance is noble, but it isn't peace."

The Mind added quietly, "And achievement isn't fulfillment."

The Body looked at both of them. "Then what is?"

The Soul smiled. "It's the space where all three of us breathe together — without rush, without resistance, without fear."

They sat in silence, feeling the truth of those words.

The Morning After

The next morning, as dawn brushed the sky with light, they awoke renewed.
The Body stretched slowly, testing its strength. The Mind, for once, didn't rush it.
The Soul simply watched, peaceful and grateful.

When they began to walk again, something was different.
The Mind no longer walked ahead — it walked *beside* the Body.
The Soul no longer trailed behind — it walked with them, in the center, like a quiet pulse that kept their rhythm steady.

The road was the same.
But now, it felt softer under their feet.

🌼 The Lesson of Loss

That day, as they walked, the Mind asked softly, "Soul, why do we have to lose something before we realize its value?"

The Soul smiled. "Because loss has a voice that success doesn't."

The Body nodded. "It's strange — I thought stopping was failure. But it was actually the first time I truly felt alive again."

The Soul's eyes glimmered with quiet wisdom. "When we rest, we listen. When we listen, we reconnect. When we reconnect, we heal. That is how the journey continues."

The Mind thought deeply. "Maybe the journey isn't about how far we go — it's about how whole we remain while going."

The Soul touched both their hands. "Yes. That's the real meaning of movement."

And as the sun rose higher, the three friends walked once again — not perfectly in sync, but lovingly aware of each other's rhythm.
It wasn't perfection anymore. It was partnership.

💭 Coach's Journal

Every journey has a moment when something — or someone — falls behind.
In the language of life, it could be your **Body** slowing down after years of overwork,
your **Mind** overwhelmed by constant pressure,
or your **Soul** silenced by noise and distraction.

And most of us respond just like the Mind did — by denying, rationalizing, or pushing harder.
We call it "staying strong." But in truth, it's how we drift apart from ourselves.

In my coaching work, I've often witnessed this silent separation.
People who have achieved success but lost the joy of living it.
Bodies that ache while minds chase goals.
Souls that whisper, "Remember me," beneath layers of noise.

The turning point always comes when awareness replaces speed.
When we pause long enough to notice what part of us has been left behind.

You don't always need to go back miles — sometimes a single pause is enough to bridge the gap.
The journey becomes lighter when all of you walks together.

So, if a part of you feels left behind today — your energy, your focus, your calm — don't judge it.
Just turn around, as the Mind did, and go back.

You'll find that your lost self was never truly gone — it was waiting patiently for you to return.

Pause & Reflect

- What part of me has been asking for rest — and have I been listening?
- Do I equate slowing down with failure?
- How do I respond when I feel one part of me falling behind — do I push harder or pause gently?

Try this:

Tonight, before bed, place your hand on your chest and breathe slowly.
Ask yourself:
"Dear Body, how are you?"
"Dear Mind, what are you holding onto?"
"Dear Soul, what do you need me to hear?"

Listen. Don't answer. Just listen.
The first step to reunion is not running back — it's *listening back.*

CHAPTER 5

THE SILENCE BETWEEN STEPS: LISTENING AGAIN

The next few days unfolded gently, like dawn stretching across a quiet sky.

After their reunion beneath the banyan tree, the three friends walked slowly — not out of weakness, but out of choice.

Each step was deliberate, each pause sacred.

The Body, still tender but healing, felt gratitude in every breath.

The Mind, humbled and quieter, was beginning to see the beauty in slowing down.

And the Soul — radiant as ever — guided them not with words, but with presence.

The road wound through meadows where tall grass whispered like prayer beads.

Birds sang unseen songs. The wind moved softly, as though careful not to disturb their new rhythm.

No one spoke for a long while. And yet, for the first time in weeks, everything felt deeply connected.

The Gift of Quiet

On the third morning, they reached a small lake.
The water was still — so still that the sky seemed to rest within it.
They stopped, not out of exhaustion, but instinct.

The Soul spoke softly. "Let's stay here for a while."

The Mind looked around. "But there's nothing here — no village, no food, no destination."

The Soul smiled. "Exactly. Nothing here is sometimes everything we need."
The Body sat by the lake and dipped its feet into the cool water. A deep sigh escaped its lips.
"This," it whispered, "feels like medicine."

The Mind hesitated but joined in, sitting beside the Body.
For once, it didn't reach for maps or plans. It simply looked — at the water, at the reflection, at the stillness that seemed to breathe back at them.

They sat together in silence.
At first, the silence felt awkward — too open, too unfamiliar.
But gradually, it began to feel like home.

The Mind's Restlessness

After some time, the Mind shifted uncomfortably.
"I'm trying to enjoy this," it confessed, "but it feels like I should be doing something."

The Soul looked at it gently. "Who taught you that doing is more valuable than being?"

The Mind paused. "Everyone, I suppose. The world moves fast. It rewards movement, not stillness."

The Soul nodded. "And yet, it is in stillness that you truly meet yourself."

The Body added, "Silence scares the Mind because it cannot control it. But silence heals the Body because it needs no control."

The Mind sighed. "I've spent so long trying to think my way to peace."

The Soul smiled. "Peace doesn't come through thought. It appears when thought finally rests."
For a long moment, no one said anything more.
The silence deepened — not empty, but full of unseen understanding.

The Language of Stillness

As dusk fell, the lake mirrored the colors of the sky — rose, amber, indigo. The Body lay back on the grass. The Mind watched the fading light. The Soul closed its eyes in quiet prayer.

And then something remarkable happened.
The Mind, for the first time in its life, stopped thinking.
Not because it was forced to, but because it no longer needed to.
It simply… rested.

In that stillness, the Body's heartbeat and the Soul's rhythm seemed to align — three distinct notes merging into one silent chord.

No words. No effort. Just presence.

Hours passed, or maybe minutes — time itself had dissolved.

When the stars appeared, the Mind whispered softly, "I feel… light."

The Soul replied, "That's because you've finally stopped carrying everything alone."

The Body smiled. "And because you're listening — not just to thoughts, but to life itself."

They stayed by the lake through the night, wrapped in the warmth of peace.

🌙 The Whisper of Awareness

At dawn, the first bird called out — a sound so gentle it felt like a continuation of silence.
The Soul stirred and said, "This stillness is not an end. It's a reminder."

The Mind tilted its head. "A reminder of what?"

"That everything we've been chasing," said the Soul, "has always been right here — beneath the noise."

The Body nodded slowly. "I think I understand. When we walk too fast, we step over the quiet places where joy is hiding."

The Mind looked out at the water, thoughtful.
"I used to think silence meant emptiness. Now I see it's full — full of understanding, full of truth."

The Soul smiled. "Yes. Silence doesn't take things away — it gives them space to be seen."

They sat together again, saying nothing.
And in that nothingness, they felt complete.

🌼 The World Returns

Eventually, it was time to move again.
The Body stood, stretching gently. The Mind gathered its thoughts — not as tools, but as companions.
The Soul rose last, eyes still soft from meditation.

As they began walking, everything around them seemed more alive — the sound of leaves, the warmth of sunlight, even the crunch of gravel beneath their feet.

The Body felt lighter, stronger.
The Mind clearer, quieter.
The Soul — as always — peaceful, but now radiant with joy.

They didn't rush. They didn't plan. They simply moved — one step, one breath, one heartbeat at a time.

🪶 The Reflection in the Water

A few miles later, they passed a small stream.
The Mind, feeling curious, leaned over to look at their reflection.

It saw three faces — tired yet glowing.
And for the first time, it noticed how similar they looked.

"Do you see this?" said the Mind softly. "We're not so different after all."

The Body laughed. "We never were. You just looked away too often."

The Soul added, "Harmony doesn't mean sameness — it means remembering that difference is divine."

The Mind nodded. "I think I finally understand. I used to speak loudly, trying to lead. But now I realize the quiet voice inside me — the one I used to ignore — was wisdom all along."

The Soul smiled, eyes bright with compassion.
"That quiet voice," it said, "is life speaking through you."

🌙 The Return of Clarity

As twilight descended, they reached a clearing and set up camp.

The Body prepared a small fire, the Mind gathered twigs, and the Soul hummed softly — a song that seemed to belong to the wind itself.

The Mind looked into the fire and said quietly, "I feel something I haven't felt in a long time — calm, without reason."

The Body nodded. "I feel strength without strain."

The Soul added, "And I feel joy without cause."

The three looked at each other and smiled.
No one spoke after that — they didn't need to.
The silence said everything.

💭 Coach's Journal

Silence is one of life's most misunderstood teachers.
We often think of it as the absence of sound or movement, but in truth, it is the presence of awareness.

In silence, we meet ourselves again — beneath the noise, beneath the expectations, beneath the endless doing.

I've seen this moment countless times in coaching — when a client stops talking mid-sentence, breathes deeply, and says, "I just realized something."
That realization doesn't come from new information; it comes from space.

The **Body** heals in stillness.
The **Mind** finds clarity in stillness.
The **Soul** reveals itself in stillness.

But silence can be uncomfortable, especially at first.
The Mind resists it, the Body fidgets, and the Soul waits patiently.
Yet, the moment we stop fighting the quiet, we begin to hear what's been waiting all along.

Silence is not a break from the journey — it *is* the journey's wisdom speaking softly.
If you can sit with silence long enough, it will tell you everything you need to know.

🌼 Pause & Reflect

- How comfortable am I with silence — with moments when nothing "seems" to be happening?
- What have I been avoiding hearing beneath the noise of my busy days?
- Can I allow quiet moments to be not interruptions, but invitations?

Try this:

Take five minutes today to practice stillness.
No phone, no music, no task.
Just breathe and notice.

You may feel restless at first. That's okay.
Stay with it.
Because silence is not empty — it's full of the answers your Soul has been waiting to give you.

CHAPTER 6

THE MEETING POINT: REDISCOVERING EACH OTHER

The morning after their time by the still lake was soft and golden.
The path ahead curved through wildflowers and light mist.
The three friends — Body, Mind, and Soul — walked together again, but this time something had changed.

Their pace was slower, their steps in rhythm, their breaths aligned.
There was no rush, no need to prove anything.
They were simply *present.*

Every sound — birds, wind, footsteps — seemed part of the same song.
The Body felt the world through sensation,
the Mind through awareness,
the Soul through gratitude.
And between the three, a new harmony began to bloom.

The Bridge of Awareness

By noon, they reached a wide river. Its surface shimmered like glass, reflecting clouds that drifted lazily across the sky.
They stopped at the edge.

The Mind spoke first, quietly: "This feels like a bridge — not of wood or stone, but of awareness."

The Soul smiled. "You're beginning to see."

The Body dipped its hands into the cool water. "It's clear," it said. "You can see right to the bottom."

The Soul nodded. "That's what happens when water is still — it reveals everything."

They stood together in silence, each feeling that truth ripple within.
The Mind realized that clarity wasn't something to be achieved — it was something to be uncovered by stillness.
The Body understood that rest wasn't weakness — it was wisdom in disguise.
The Soul simply watched them both with joy, sensing they were finally listening.

🌸 The Apology

The Mind turned toward the Body, voice trembling slightly.
"I owe you an apology," it said. "For all the times I pushed you past your limits — telling you to keep going when you needed to stop."

The Body smiled gently. "And I owe you forgiveness. Without your vision, I might never have moved at all. We both did what we thought was right."

The Soul added softly, "Love often looks like forgiveness in motion."

The Mind looked to the Soul. "And you… I doubted you. I called you slow, impractical, abstract. I was wrong. You're the reason we're still walking."

The Soul's eyes glimmered like the river's surface. "And you're the reason we learned how."

For a moment, none of them spoke. They didn't need to. The river carried their silence forward — turning regret into reconciliation.

The Meeting Point

They followed the river until it widened into a gentle bend.
There, beneath a large peepal tree, stood a stone with three grooves crossing at its center.

The Soul stopped and said, "This is it — the meeting point."

The Body and Mind looked at each other. "Meeting point?" the Mind asked.

The Soul smiled. "The place where all our paths overlap. The moment when we stop seeing ourselves as separate."

They sat beneath the tree — Body, Mind, and Soul — in quiet awareness.

The Body said, "I feel alive again."
The Mind said, "I feel clear."
The Soul said, "I feel whole."

And together, they realized they had found something far greater than rest — **they had found rhythm.**

The Understanding

As afternoon light filtered through the leaves, the Soul spoke again.

"You see," it said, "our journey was never about reaching a destination. It was about remembering who we are to one another."

The Body nodded. "I am your foundation — the vessel through which experience flows."

The Mind added, "I am your compass — the lens that gives direction."

And the Soul completed, "And I am your essence — the stillness that holds it all together."

The three looked at one another, smiling, tears glinting softly.
They had walked many miles, climbed many hills, and faced many storms.
But the most important distance they had traveled was inward — from separation to unity.

🌙 The Evening Lesson

That evening, as they rested by the riverbank, the Body began to hum a tune — deep, grounding.
The Mind, usually quick to analyze, just listened.
The Soul joined softly, turning the hum into a melody that seemed older than memory.

It was simple — three notes repeating, rising and falling together.
And yet, in that simplicity was everything: movement, thought, and meaning — perfectly aligned.

The Mind laughed suddenly. "Do you hear that? We've made music!"

The Soul smiled. "Yes. And the world has been waiting to hear it."

The Body added, "It feels different this time — not performance, not pressure — just pure joy."

They looked at one another and realized: this was what they had been seeking all along.
Not the mountain or the map. Not success or rest.
But this — *belonging within themselves.*

The Awakening Within

Later that night, while stars shimmered above, the Mind lay awake, thinking softly — but not restlessly.
It turned to the Soul and whispered, "How will we remember this harmony when life becomes noisy again?"

The Soul replied, "By listening — not to the world, but to the space between your own thoughts."

The Mind nodded slowly. "And what if I forget?"

The Soul smiled. "Then the Body will remind you — through fatigue, tension, or discomfort. Pain is often the Body's way of saying, 'You're walking alone again.'"

The Mind smiled at that truth. "So even pain is a teacher."

"Yes," said the Soul. "Every part of you wants the same thing — togetherness."

The Body murmured sleepily, "Then let's promise to remember this feeling — not by holding on to it, but by returning to it whenever we drift."

The Soul whispered, "That's the secret. The meeting point is not a place — it's a practice."

Coach's Journal

This chapter of our inner journey — the rediscovery of alignment — mirrors the moment when awareness returns after long imbalance.

In coaching conversations, I often see this as a *shift from doing to being.* When a client pauses long enough to connect with what their body feels, what their mind believes, and what their heart knows, something profound happens — not externally, but internally.

Harmony doesn't mean everything is perfect. It means everything is heard.
The **Body** speaks through sensation,
the **Mind** through thought,
the **Soul** through intuition.

When these voices overlap, you experience *clarity without strain.*
That's the real "meeting point."
You don't need to find it once — you need to return to it often.
Like breathing, awareness isn't permanent; it's rhythmic.
It's a conversation that keeps you whole.

So, whenever you feel scattered, pause and ask:
"Where are my three friends right now?"
"Are they walking together?"

That single question can bring you back home.

🏵 Pause & Reflect

- When was the last time I felt truly in sync — physically, mentally, and spiritually?
- What does my personal "meeting point" look like in daily life?
- How can I nurture harmony among my Body, Mind, and Soul when life becomes chaotic?

Try this:

Before starting any important task, take 60 seconds to check in with yourself:

Body — Am I comfortable?
Mind — Am I clear?
Soul — Am I at peace?

If even one answers “no,” pause and adjust.
Your success doesn’t depend on how much you do, but on how whole you are while doing it.

PART III

THE REUNION: WHEN LIFE FEELS WHOLE AGAIN

CHAPTER 7

THE JOURNEY IN HARMONY: LEARNING TO WALK TOGETHER

The sun rose slowly that morning, as though honoring their quiet transformation.
Mist lingered over the fields, and each droplet of dew shimmered with light — small worlds reflecting the vastness of the sky.

The three friends — Body, Mind, and Soul — began walking again.
But now, their steps were different.
No one led. No one followed.
They moved as one — three parts of the same melody, flowing effortlessly through the rhythm of life.

🌿 The Dance of Balance

The Body walked with awareness now.
It listened to its own signals — the pull of a muscle, the thirst for water, the warmth of sunlight.
No longer a vehicle of ambition, it had become a teacher of presence.

The Mind, too, had softened.
It still planned, still imagined, but now its thoughts were shaped by compassion.

It no longer raced ahead or criticized the pace.
Instead, it asked gentle questions: "Is this the right moment?" "Does this feel true?"

And the Soul — ever patient — glowed quietly between them, like the space between notes in a song.
It didn't guide through words anymore, but through silence — through the grace of simply being.

Together, they had discovered something profound:

Harmony is not the absence of struggle, but the presence of listening.

❀ The Test of Flow

A few days later, they reached a vast meadow where the road split in two.
One path was short and straight, leading through the valley.
The other was long and winding, leading up a gentle hill.

The Mind immediately analyzed. "The shorter path will save time and energy."
The Body, remembering its earlier fatigue, said, "The longer path looks peaceful — easier on my steps."
The Soul smiled. "Then let's pause before deciding."

They sat beneath a tree and watched both roads in silence.
A breeze passed softly through the grass.
The Mind exhaled. "Why does it feel so hard to choose when both paths seem right?"

The Soul replied, "Because you're trying to choose with thought, not with awareness."

The Body nodded slowly. "Maybe we don't need to pick the 'best' path — just the one that feels true."

The Soul smiled. "Exactly. Harmony means moving not from logic or comfort alone, but from *alignment.*"

After a few quiet moments, the Mind closed its eyes and listened — not to reason, but to rhythm.
When it opened them again, it said softly, "I think the longer path is calling us."

The Body grinned. "Then let's go."
And the Soul whispered, "You've just chosen with your whole being."

Walking in Rhythm

The hill path turned out to be beautiful — wildflowers blooming on either side, streams crossing their way, the scent of pine in the air.

They moved steadily, stopping whenever the Body needed to breathe or the Mind wanted to reflect.
There was no pressure to move faster, no guilt in slowing down.
Each pause was simply part of the journey.

Sometimes the Body led, full of strength and enthusiasm.
Sometimes the Mind guided, offering direction and insight.
And sometimes the Soul took over, reminding them to rest and watch the sky.

They were no longer three travelers — they were *a single consciousness in motion.*

The Lesson of Flow

One afternoon, as they walked through a narrow valley, it began to rain.
At first, the Mind grew anxious. "We should find shelter. We'll get soaked!"

The Body looked up at the sky, feeling the cool drops. "It's just rain. My skin was made for this."

The Soul smiled. "What if we didn't resist? What if we simply walked with it?"

So they did.

They walked through the rain — slow, steady, laughing.
The water washed away the dust of old journeys, the tension of old fears.

When they reached the next clearing, the rain stopped, and sunlight poured through the clouds like a blessing.

The Mind laughed. "I didn't realize how freeing it feels not to control everything."

The Body stretched its arms wide. "And how alive I feel when I just let go."

The Soul said quietly, "That's what flow feels like — effort melting into ease."

And at that moment, they understood something essential:

Life doesn't always need managing. Sometimes it just needs *allowing*.

🌙 Harmony in Action

That evening, they came across a small village. The people there were kind but busy — rushing about, chasing their own goals and burdens.

The Body helped an old woman carry water.
The Mind listened to a young man's worries and offered gentle guidance.
The Soul sat with a child, watching the sunset in silence.

Each one served in its own way, and yet all were connected by the same quiet intention: presence.

When they left the village, the Mind said softly, "I used to think harmony was something to keep for myself. But it's meant to be shared."

The Soul nodded. "When you walk in balance, your steps become medicine for others."

The Body smiled. "Then our journey is no longer just ours — it's everyone's who walks beside us, even for a while."

🪶 The Return of Laughter

For the first time in a long time, they began to laugh again — not from excitement, but from peace.
It was the laughter of lightness, of understanding, of freedom.

The Mind laughed at its old seriousness.
The Body laughed at how it had once confused exhaustion with achievement.
The Soul laughed softly at how both had forgotten that joy is not a reward — it's a companion.

They laughed until the stars appeared, and even then, the sound of their joy lingered in the air like music.

🌙 The Night Reflection

As they sat by the campfire that night, the Soul spoke softly.
"We've walked through conflict, silence, and reconciliation. Now we're learning the real art — the art of walking together."

The Mind nodded. "It's not as hard as I thought. I just have to listen more than I plan."

The Body stretched, smiling. "And I just have to rest before I break."

The Soul chuckled. "And I just have to keep reminding you both that we were never separate."

They looked at one another, their faces glowing in the firelight.
The Body's strength, the Mind's clarity, and the Soul's calm — all reflecting in one flame.

The night sky stretched endlessly above them.
For the first time, they felt not like travelers, but like home itself.

💭 Coach's Journal

Harmony is not a destination — it's a daily practice of listening inward. When your Body, Mind, and Soul begin to move together, life doesn't suddenly become easy — it becomes *clear.*

The **Body** tells you when to rest and when to rise.
The **Mind** guides you through choices, bringing focus.
The **Soul** connects it all with meaning.

When they work together, even ordinary actions — a walk, a conversation, a breath — become sacred.

But remember: balance is not constant. It's rhythmic.
You'll drift, then return; rush, then rest; disconnect, then rediscover.
And that's okay. The beauty lies not in staying perfectly centered, but in noticing when you've moved away — and choosing to come back.

Harmony isn't found through control.
It's found through awareness — through your willingness to listen again, and again, and again.

🌼 Pause & Reflect

- Where in my life do I feel in harmony — where things flow naturally without effort?

- What part of me needs more listening — my Body, my Mind, or my Soul?
- How can I bring more presence into everyday actions like walking, eating, or working?

Try this:

Tomorrow morning, as you walk — even if it's just across a room — walk slowly, consciously.
Notice your feet touch the ground.
Feel your breath.
Let your thoughts move like gentle ripples, not waves.

That's what it means to walk in harmony — not perfectly, but peacefully.

CHAPTER 8

THE UNEXPECTED DETOURS: LIFE'S TESTS

The road was smooth again, and the days unfolded with a peaceful rhythm.
The three friends — Body, Mind, and Soul — had found their flow.
Each step was steady, each silence filled with ease.

But harmony is a delicate thing.
It is not a fortress built to resist life — it's a river that must keep flowing through it.
And one day, life decided to test that flow.

The Detour Appears

They had planned to follow the river until it met the mountains.
But one afternoon, the path ahead was blocked by a fallen tree — massive, unmovable, roots torn out by a recent storm.

The Body stopped first. "We can't cross here," it said.

The Mind frowned, calculating. "We can go around, but that'll add a day, maybe two."

The Soul looked at the tree quietly. "Then perhaps the tree is here for a reason."

The Mind sighed. "Everything doesn't have to be symbolic, you know."

The Soul smiled. "Maybe not. But everything has something to teach."

The Body nodded thoughtfully. "So what now? Do we climb, wait, or change direction?"

The Mind thought for a long time, then said, "Let's find another way. There's always a shortcut."

The Soul whispered, "And sometimes, the shortcut becomes the long way home."

The New Path

They decided to follow a smaller trail that veered off to the left.
It was narrow, uneven, and unfamiliar — nothing like the calm road they'd grown used to.

The Body soon felt the strain — stones bruising its feet, branches scratching its skin.
The Mind grew restless — uncertain of where the path would lead.
The Soul, though quiet, began to hum a low, comforting tune.

Hours passed. The sun sank lower. They were still walking.

"This doesn't feel right," said the Mind. "We've lost direction."

The Body groaned, "We've lost energy."

The Soul said softly, "Maybe we're not lost — maybe we're being rerouted."

The Mind rolled its eyes. "Spiritual logic won't get us anywhere!"

But the Soul didn't argue. It simply walked on, eyes open, presence steady.

The First Sign of Doubt

By evening, they reached a rocky clearing.
The Body collapsed onto the ground, muscles aching.
The Mind paced back and forth, frustrated.

"This is a waste of time," it said. "We had a rhythm, a plan, and now it's gone."

The Soul sat down beside the Body and said quietly, "Sometimes plans have to break for wisdom to grow."

The Mind turned sharply. "Wisdom doesn't feed hunger or find shelter!"

The Soul replied calmly, "No. But it teaches us to see beyond what hunger and fear hide."

The Mind fell silent, anger slowly dissolving into exhaustion.

The Body looked at them both and whispered, "Maybe it's okay not to know where we're going."

The Soul nodded. "Yes. Because it's only when we stop knowing that we start trusting."

The Storm

That night, a storm rolled in — wild, relentless.
The wind howled through the valley, the rain lashed the earth, and thunder echoed like the world's heartbeat.

They took shelter beneath a rocky ledge.
The Body shivered, the Mind panicked, and the Soul remained still — not out of control, but out of surrender.

"This is madness," said the Mind. "We should've stayed on the main road!"

The Body clenched its fists. "We couldn't — the tree blocked us!"

The Soul spoke softly through the storm. "Maybe the storm is not against us. Maybe it's cleansing us."

"Cleansing?" the Mind shouted. "We're cold, wet, and lost!"

"Yes," the Soul said gently, "and alive."

The Mind fell quiet. Something about that truth pierced its fear.

They sat together in silence, huddled close, letting the storm rage above them.

After the Rain

By morning, the world was unrecognizable — washed clean, fresh, alive again.
The air smelled of earth and beginnings.
The Body stretched, sore but strong.
The Mind looked out at the mist rising from the ground, eyes soft.
The Soul smiled, as though it had been expecting this moment.

The Mind finally said, "I was afraid all night. But now that it's over, I see something I didn't before."

"What's that?" asked the Body.

"That fear doesn't disappear when the storm ends. It disappears when you stop running from it."

The Soul nodded approvingly. "Yes. Peace is not the absence of storms, but the courage to stand through them."

The Body chuckled. "Then we passed the test?"

The Soul smiled. "The test wasn't whether you'd survive — it was whether you'd stay together."

🌼 The Unexpected Gift

As they resumed walking, they noticed that the storm had cleared the fallen tree from the original path.
The road was open again.

The Mind stared in disbelief. "We could've just waited?"

The Soul smiled knowingly. "Sometimes waiting takes more strength than walking."

The Body nodded. "And sometimes what we call delay is simply divine timing."

The Mind sighed, half laughing. "So the detour wasn't a mistake after all."

The Soul placed a hand on the Mind's shoulder. "There are no mistakes in a journey walked with awareness — only lessons disguised as detours."

They stood together in silence, looking at the open road.
It felt familiar, yet new — as though the storm had not only changed the landscape, but also changed them.

🌙 Walking with Wisdom

As they continued, their steps were slower but deeper — each footfall a reminder of resilience.
The Body had learned endurance without force.
The Mind had learned humility without defeat.
And the Soul — ever radiant — had taught them both that even chaos can be sacred.

They no longer feared the unexpected.
Instead, they began to see every twist, every delay, every discomfort as an invitation to trust more deeply.

The Mind said, "I think I finally understand. The purpose of the journey isn't to control what happens — it's to grow through it."

The Body added, "And to stay kind to ourselves while doing so."

The Soul smiled. "That's harmony in motion — awareness through uncertainty."

The Evening Insight

That evening, as they camped under a clear sky, the stars glimmered brighter than ever.
The Body rested peacefully, the Mind watched the stars, and the Soul whispered softly, "Every detour is a doorway."

The Mind turned to it. "A doorway to what?"

"To yourself," said the Soul. "Because in uncertainty, the only compass that truly works is awareness."

The Mind nodded slowly. "Maybe the storm wasn't sent to stop us — it was sent to wake us."

The Soul smiled. "Exactly. Life never tests us to break us. It tests us to show us where we've stopped listening."

The Body murmured sleepily, "Then I hope we keep listening — even when it rains."

The Soul looked at the stars. "And even when it's silent."

Coach's Journal

Life's detours are not punishments — they're invitations.
Invitations to slow down, reorient, and deepen trust.

In every coaching journey, there's a moment when progress seems to stall.

Clients say, "I thought I was doing so well, and then everything fell apart." But when we pause and look closely, those moments aren't breakdowns — they're breakthroughs in disguise.

The **Body** reminds us that growth requires recovery.
The **Mind** learns to release its obsession with control.
The **Soul** teaches surrender — not as giving up, but as giving *in* to the flow of life.

When the unexpected comes — illness, loss, delay, change — ask not "Why is this happening?" but "What is this teaching me about trust?"
Every detour is part of your design.
You were never off-track; you were just being redirected toward depth.

🏵 Pause & Reflect

- How do I respond when life takes an unexpected turn — with resistance or curiosity?
- What detour in my past turned out to be a hidden blessing?
- Where can I practice trusting the process instead of fighting it?

Try this:

When something doesn't go as planned today, pause.
Take one conscious breath and whisper to yourself:

"Maybe this, too, has a reason I can't see yet."

You'll be surprised how quickly peace returns when you choose trust over tension.

CHAPTER 9

THE COACH ARRIVES: MEETING THE OBSERVER

The morning began like any other.
The road stretched ahead, calm and familiar, lined with soft hills and scattered trees.
The Body, Mind, and Soul walked together, steady in rhythm, grateful for the harmony they'd rediscovered.

The air was cool, the sky clear — it felt like peace itself had decided to walk with them.
But that day, something subtle began to shift.
A quiet awareness entered their steps — something beyond thought, beyond feeling, beyond being.

It wasn't visible, but it was present.
And as they moved, each of them began to sense it.

🌿 A Presence Between Them

The Body felt it first — a soft stillness inside.
Its steps felt guided, not by effort but by intuition.
It wasn't walking *for* the Mind or the Soul anymore; it was walking *with* something deeper.

The Mind noticed it next — a pause between thoughts, a quiet observer that watched even as it planned and reasoned.
It wasn't judgmental; it was simply aware.

And the Soul — who had always known — smiled softly and whispered, "Ah, you've finally met the Coach."

The Body turned curiously. "The Coach?"

"Yes," said the Soul. "The one who's been with us from the beginning — watching, waiting, guiding silently."

The Mind frowned. "But we've never seen anyone else on this path."

The Soul chuckled. "That's because the Coach isn't outside of us. It lives within."

The Meeting

As they continued walking, the presence grew stronger — not in form, but in feeling.
It was like walking with a mirror that reflected everything without distortion.

The Body spoke softly, "I feel… seen. As if something inside me understands my pain and effort."

The Mind added, "And I feel calmer. Like my thoughts are being heard without interruption."

The Soul smiled. "That's what the Coach does — it listens without agenda, sees without judgment."

They stopped by a quiet meadow and sat beneath a large tree.
The air felt unusually still — as though the world was holding its breath for them to notice.

And then they heard it — not a voice, but a vibration within, gentle and profound.

"I have always been here," it said.
"When you argued, I listened.
When you fell, I held you.
When you silenced yourselves, I whispered.
I am the space between you — the awareness that connects what you think, what you feel, and what you are."

The Body closed its eyes, tears forming. "I thought I was alone in my exhaustion."

"You were never alone," said the voice. "You were just unheard — even by yourself."

The Mind lowered its gaze. "I thought I was in control."

"Control is useful," said the voice, "but awareness is freedom."

The Soul smiled softly. "I knew you would speak when they were ready."

"And now you all are," said the voice.

The Realization

For the first time, the three friends understood that the journey had never been *just theirs*.
There had always been something larger walking beside them — the quiet consciousness that observed without trying to interfere.

It was The Coach — the *inner witness*, the awareness that exists beyond roles, beyond doing.

The Mind asked curiously, "Then what is your role? Are you here to teach us?"

"No," said the Coach. "I am not here to teach — only to remind. You already know. My role is to help you remember."

The Body asked, "Remember what?"

"That you are not separate parts," the voice replied.
"You are expressions of the same life.
The Body experiences,
the Mind interprets,
the Soul illuminates —
but I am the awareness that allows all of it to exist."

A long silence followed. The Body, Mind, and Soul sat quietly, letting the truth settle.

It wasn't a lesson. It was a homecoming.

The Mirror Within

The Mind spoke again, softly. "If you are awareness, then have you been here even when we made mistakes?"

"Especially then," said the Coach. "Awareness never leaves; it only waits for recognition."

The Body asked, "Why didn't we notice you before?"

"Because you were busy trying to fix yourselves. Awareness doesn't compete with noise; it waits beneath it."

The Soul whispered, "That's why silence felt so healing — it was the space where you could finally hear the Coach."

The Mind nodded slowly. "So this is the true journey — not from place to place, but from distraction to awareness."

"Exactly," said the Coach. "When you remember me, your steps become light. When you forget, life reminds you gently — through pain, through pause, through people."

The Body smiled. "Then every ache, every challenge, every detour — it was all you calling us back?"

"Yes," said the Coach. "Life itself is a conversation between your awareness and your forgetting."

The Return of Wholeness

As the sun began to set, the three friends felt a peace unlike any they had known before — not the fleeting calm of rest, but the deep stillness of understanding.

The Body felt strong but not burdened.
The Mind felt active but not anxious.
The Soul felt radiant but not distant.

All three were now moving in harmony under the gentle gaze of the Coach — the observer within.

The Body said softly, "So our journey has been inward all along."

"Always," said the Coach. "The world outside is just a reflection of your inner movement."

The Mind smiled. "Then awareness is like light — it doesn't stop the shadows, but it helps us see them clearly."

"And seeing is enough," said the Coach. "Healing begins when you stop fighting what is."

The Soul whispered, "You've been the silence behind our songs."

"And you," said the Coach, "have been my voice in motion."

The Body, Mind, and Soul smiled.
They realized that the Coach was not a visitor, not a teacher — it was *who they had always been beneath their names.*

A New Way of Walking

That night, they walked again under the stars.
But now, their journey had a new depth — every step felt guided by invisible wisdom.

The Body noticed the ground beneath its feet as alive.
The Mind saw thoughts as clouds drifting through a vast sky.
The Soul felt joy simply existing in the present moment.

And through all of it, the Coach — silent awareness — smiled within, watching, loving, holding.

The Soul turned inward and whispered, "Thank you."

"No," said the Coach, "thank *you* — for finally listening."

Coach's Journal

The "Coach" in this story is not a person.
It's the awareness that each of us carries — the part of you that observes your thoughts, emotions, and sensations without judgment.

In coaching, we call this *the observer self* — the inner space that notices before reacting.
When this awareness awakens, you stop living reactively and start living consciously.

You begin to see your **Body** as your ally, not your limit.
Your **Mind** as your instrument, not your identity.
Your **Soul** as your compass, not your escape.

This awareness is what allows transformation to happen.
It doesn't force; it invites.
It doesn't instruct; it illuminates.

The role of every external coach — including me — is not to give answers, but to awaken this inner coach in you.
Because once you hear its voice, you'll never be truly lost again.

Pause & Reflect

- Can I notice the "observer" within me right now — the part that watches thoughts and feelings without reacting?
- How often do I pause before responding to what happens in my life?
- What might change if I treated awareness itself as my inner guide?

Try this:

Take a few minutes each day to sit quietly.
Close your eyes and notice your breath.
Then, instead of controlling it, just *watch it.*
When thoughts come, notice them — "thinking."
When sensations come, notice them — "feeling."
That awareness — steady, kind, nonjudgmental — *is* your Coach.

Listen to it often.
It has been waiting for you to remember.

CHAPTER 10

THE HAPPY JOURNEY: ARRIVING WITHOUT ARRIVING

The morning light spread across the valley like a soft smile.
The road ahead was neither long nor short, familiar nor strange — it simply *was*.

The Body, Mind, and Soul walked together, but something was beautifully different now.
They no longer felt like travelers trying to reach somewhere.
Each step felt like home.

The Body was strong, but unhurried.
The Mind was alert, but quiet.
The Soul was luminous, but humble.
And walking silently with them — as always — was the Coach, the quiet awareness that had watched every step.

The Illusion of Arrival

As they reached a wide open field, the Mind asked softly, "So, is this it? Have we finally arrived?"

The Soul smiled. "Arrived where?"

"At peace," said the Mind. "At the end of our journey."

The Soul chuckled. "Peace is not a place we arrive at, my friend. It's the way we travel."

The Body nodded. "Then we've been arriving all along — with every step."

The Coach's voice — soft and steady — filled the air:
"Yes. Every breath that's taken with awareness is arrival.
Every moment lived in harmony is home."

The Mind reflected quietly. "Then all this time, I was chasing what was walking beside me."

"Exactly," said the Coach. "You were never lost. You were just busy measuring the way."

They laughed gently, the kind of laughter that comes from relief — the kind that sounds like gratitude.

The Joy of Being

They sat under a large tree as a breeze danced through the leaves.
The Body leaned back, feeling the earth's pulse beneath it.
The Mind watched the play of light and shadow.
The Soul hummed softly — a tune that sounded like stillness made audible.

After a while, the Body said, "Do you remember when we used to rush? Every day was a chase."

The Mind nodded. "And every pause felt like failure."

The Soul smiled. "But without those moments, we wouldn't have learned to listen."

The Coach spoke quietly:
"Growth often looks like slowing down.
Awareness feels like less doing, but deeper being."

The Body said, "So the goal was never to reach the mountain, but to walk awake."

"Yes," said the Coach. "To realize that life doesn't happen ahead of you — it happens within you."

They sat for a long while, feeling this truth ripple through them.
The journey had not given them something new — it had simply revealed what had always been there.

🌼 A New Way of Seeing

As the sun began to set, they resumed walking.
But the world looked different now — or perhaps they were finally seeing it as it truly was.

The trees weren't just trees; they were breathing.
The wind wasn't just movement; it was a message.
Every sound, every color, every silence felt connected.

The Body felt it first — "I belong here," it whispered.
The Mind followed — "I understand now."
And the Soul glowed — "I have always known."

The Coach's voice came again, softer than before:

"This is what wholeness feels like — not perfection, but participation.
To live in awareness is to walk in joy, no matter the road."

The Body smiled. "Even when it rains?"

"Especially when it rains," said the Coach.

They laughed together, and for a brief, timeless moment, laughter and silence felt like the same thing.

🌙 The Circle Completes

That evening, as they reached a small hilltop, they saw something in the distance — the same horizon they had left behind so long ago.
The path had brought them full circle.

The Body gasped softly. "We've come back to where we began."

The Mind looked closer. "Yes — but everything looks different now."

The Soul smiled. "That's because *we're* different."

The Coach added,

"Journeys don't change the world. They change the eyes that see it."
The three friends stood there quietly, watching the golden light fade into dusk.
There was no sense of completion, no need for closure.
Only gratitude — deep, wordless gratitude.

The Body whispered, "Thank you, Mind, for your focus."
The Mind replied, "Thank you, Body, for your endurance."
And both turned to the Soul and said, "Thank you for your light."

The Soul bowed gently. "Thank you both for remembering me."

Then all three turned inward and said together, "And thank you, Coach — for being the silence that held us through it all."

The Coach's voice rose softly like the wind:

"You are welcome.
And remember — the happy journey is not somewhere you go.
It's who you become when you walk together."

Walking On

The night was warm, filled with starlight.
The Body walked with gentle confidence, feeling life in every step.
The Mind observed, no longer trying to control, only to understand.
The Soul radiated peace, knowing every direction now led home.

And awareness — the Coach — shimmered quietly inside them all.
The world ahead remained unknown, but the fear of the unknown had vanished.
They no longer needed a map, because they had found the rhythm of trust.

Each step, each breath, each silence was sacred.

And somewhere in the stillness, a whisper moved through the night:

"You have not reached the destination.
You have become the journey."

Coach's Journal

This is the truth every journey points toward — there is no final arrival, only deeper awareness.
We keep walking, not to escape life, but to live it more consciously.

The **Body** teaches us to inhabit the present.
The **Mind** teaches us to discern and reflect.
The **Soul** teaches us to surrender and trust.
And the **Coach** — awareness itself — teaches us to observe with compassion.

When these voices walk together, happiness stops being a goal.
It becomes a *state of being.*

You don't need to know the future to feel peace.

You only need to be fully awake to this moment — to the life happening in you, around you, and through you.

Happiness is not an end.
It's how you walk when you finally remember that there is no separation — only steps made whole by awareness.

Pause & Reflect

- Where in my life am I still chasing arrival, instead of living the journey?
- What would it feel like to see each day as a complete, sacred step rather than a means to an end?
- How can I bring more presence, kindness, and curiosity into my daily walk?

Try this:

The next time you walk — whether through a corridor, a park, or your living room — whisper to yourself:

"This is the journey."

Then take one slow, conscious breath.
Smile — not because everything is perfect, but because you are awake enough to notice.

That awareness, that smile — that's what it means to live a *happy journey.*

EPILOGUE – A LETTER FROM THE COACH

Dear Traveler,

You've walked a long way through these pages — not across miles, but through moments.

You've seen how the Body grew weary, how the Mind wandered, how the Soul waited, and how awareness — quietly, patiently — guided them home.

Now, as you close this book, I want you to pause.

Take a slow breath.

Notice the way air enters your lungs, how your chest rises and falls.

Notice how your thoughts come and go, like clouds across a vast sky.

Notice that beneath all of it, *you are here — watching, witnessing, aware.*

That witness — that still, unchanging presence — is me.

I am the Coach within you.

I Was There All Along

I was there when you took your first steps in this world — curious, brave, unafraid.

I was there when you first learned to run, to chase, to dream.

And I was there, quietly watching, when you began to believe that you had to prove yourself to keep moving.

I have walked beside you through your triumphs and your tears.

Through the noise of achievement and the silence of doubt.

Through every moment when your Body whispered "slow down,"

and your Mind shouted "not yet,"
and your Soul sighed, "Remember me."

I never interfered.
I never scolded.
Because my role was never to lead you — only to help you *see.*

The Truth About the Journey

You were never meant to choose between Body, Mind, and Soul.
They are not opposites — they are companions.
Each carries wisdom the others need.

The **Body** teaches presence — the miracle of being alive in this moment.
The **Mind** teaches purpose — the beauty of creating meaning through thought.
The **Soul** teaches peace — the grace of trusting what cannot be seen.

And I — your awareness — weave them together into one seamless experience called *you.*

When you forget me, life feels heavy.
When you remember, everything becomes light again.
Not because the road changes — but because *you do.*

You Are Not Behind

You may sometimes feel you've lost time — that others are ahead, and you've fallen behind.
But the truth is, there is no "behind."
There is only this moment, and your willingness to be present within it.

Every pause you take, every breath you notice, every gentle act of awareness is progress.

Because growth isn't measured in miles or milestones — it's measured in depth of presence.

So the next time your Mind races ahead, or your Body feels tired, or your Soul grows silent — don't panic.
Don't call it failure.
Just smile softly and say,

"Ah, we've drifted a little. Let's walk together again."

That simple remembering is all it takes to return to balance.

🏵 The Sacred Ordinary

You don't need to climb mountains or cross oceans to find meaning.
You only need to be fully alive to the small things that are already happening.

When you eat, taste it.
When you walk, feel your feet touch the earth.
When you listen, *really* listen — not to reply, but to understand.
When you rest, let it be complete, without guilt.

The sacred is not hidden in rituals or temples — it's hidden in awareness.
The divine doesn't speak in thunder; it whispers through attention.

So make your daily life your meditation.
Let your commute, your work, your laughter, your silence — all be prayers in motion.
This is what it means to live as a whole being — Body, Mind, Soul, and Awareness as one.

🌙 When You Forget — and You Will

You will forget.

You will get caught again in the rush of life, the pull of goals, the noise of others.
You will find yourself running without rhythm, working without rest, thinking without pause.

And that's okay.
Forgetting is part of remembering.
Falling out of balance is how you recognize balance when it returns.
Each time you drift, you create a new opportunity to awaken more deeply.

So don't punish yourself for forgetting.
Just return.
Return kindly, gently, with curiosity.
Awareness will always welcome you back without judgment — because it never left.

The Art of Returning

When you feel lost, do this simple practice:

1. **Pause.**
   Stop what you're doing, just for a breath.
2. **Breathe.**
   Feel the air moving in and out of your Body.
3. **Name.**
   Silently say to yourself: "This is my Body. This is my Mind. This is my Soul."
4. **Listen.**
   Ask gently: "What do you need right now?"
5. **Rejoin.**
   Take a small action — stretch, smile, rest, breathe — that honors all three.

That's it.

Five steps.
Five seconds.
And you'll return to the happy journey — to yourself.

🌼 You Are the Journey

You keep looking for purpose — but purpose is not waiting at the end of the road.
It's walking in your steps right now.

You keep seeking meaning — but meaning is in the way you live the ordinary moments.
You keep asking what makes life fulfilling —
but the answer is simple: **wholeness.**

When you live with awareness — when your Body, Mind, and Soul move as one — life becomes not a struggle to reach somewhere, but a dance you can finally enjoy.

Then, every sunrise feels like a beginning.
Every pause feels like grace.
Every breath feels like home.

That is happiness — not the emotion, but the *awareness of being alive.*

🌙 Until We Meet Again

And so, dear traveller, as you close this book, remember:
You are not at the end of a journey.
You are standing in the middle of it — where life happens, where awareness breathes, where joy quietly waits to be noticed.

Don't rush to the next thing.
Don't wait for everything to be perfect.
Just begin again — here, now, with kindness.

Walk lightly.
Listen deeply.
Breathe fully.

And whenever you forget, I will be here —
in your stillness,
in your breath,
in the space between your thoughts.

Because I am not separate from you.
I am the part of you that never stops believing, never stops observing, never stops guiding.

You don't have to look for me.
Just stop long enough to feel me.

And I promise — you'll never walk alone again.

With you, always,
— The Coach

ACKNOWLEDGMENTS

Writing this book has been a journey in itself — one that began quietly within me and unfolded through the kindness, wisdom, and support of many wonderful people.

To begin with, I offer my heartfelt gratitude to all my clients, coachees, and fellow travelers who have trusted me with their stories. Every conversation, every silence, and every reflection we shared became a thread in this book's fabric. You showed me that human growth is not a straight path but a living dialogue between courage and vulnerability.

To my mentors and teachers, thank you for guiding me with patience and depth. Your wisdom shaped not just my coaching practice but also my understanding of life's subtler rhythms. You taught me that listening truly listening — is the beginning of all transformation.

To my friends and colleagues, whose encouragement helped me believe that this story was worth telling — thank you for reminding me that creativity, like growth, thrives in connection.

To my family, whose unconditional love and faith have been my grounding force — thank you for being my constant companions through every season of life.

To my parents, who taught me the values of integrity, kindness, and humility — your blessings have been my guiding light in every step of this journey.

To my wife, Geeta, whose patience, understanding, and quiet strength have supported me in ways words can never capture — this book carries your silent grace on every page.

And to my two lovely daughters, whose love, laughter, and affection remind me daily of what joy truly means — you are my reason to keep growing, learning, and walking this happy journey.

I would also like to acknowledge the small sparks of inspiration that life offered along the way — including one evening spent watching *Zindagi Na Milegi Dobara*. That simple thought — *"What if these friends got separated? Would they still enjoy the journey?"* — planted the seed for this book.

And finally, to you, dear reader — thank you for opening these pages and walking beside me. This book finds its meaning only through your reflection and presence.

May you walk gently, listen deeply, and always remember — your Body, Mind, and Soul are lifelong friends, waiting to travel together in harmony.

Happy Journey, my friend.
— *Kishore Kumar Thakur*